HUXLEY AND EDUCATION

First published 1910
This edition published by Lector House in 2024

ISBN: 978-93-6138-003-7
Edition copyright © 2024 by Lector House LLP
All rights reserved under the International Copyright Conventions.

Every possible effort has been made to ensure that the information contained in this book is accurate at the time of going to press and the publisher cannot accept responsibility for any errors or omissions, however caused, in this unabridged, slightly corrected republication of the text of the first edition. No responsibility for loss or damage occasioned to any person, acting or refraining from action, as a result of the material in this publication can be accepted by the publisher. The publisher is not associated with any product or vendor mentioned in the book. The contents of this work are intended to further general scientific research, understanding and discussion, only. Readers should consult with a specialist, where appropriate.

No part of this publication may be reproduced, stored in a retrieval system, or transmitted, in any form, or by any means, electronic, mechanical, photocopying or otherwise, without the prior permission of the publisher.

Lector House LLP
Registered Office: H. No. 96, Block C, Tomar Colony,
Burari, Delhi – 110084, India
info@lectorhouse.com
www.lectorhouse.com

HUXLEY AND EDUCATION

HENRY FAIRFIELD OSBORN

2024

LECTOR HOUSE LLP

HUXLEY AND EDUCATION
ADDRESS AT
THE OPENING OF THE COLLEGE YEAR
COLUMBIA UNIVERSITY
SEPTEMBER 28, 1910

BY

HENRY FAIRFIELD OSBORN
LL.D., Hon. D.Sc, Camb.
DA COSTA PROFESSOR OF ZOOLOGY

Huxley and Education

"The stars come nightly to the sky;
The tidal wave comes to the sea;
Nor time, nor space, nor deep, nor high
Can keep my own away from me."

—BURROUGHS.

The most sanguine day of the college year is the opening one: the student has not yet faced the impossible task annually presented of embracing the modern world of knowledge; his errors and failures of earlier years are forgotten; he faces the coming months full of new hope.

How would my old master, Huxley, address you if he were to find you in this felicitous frame of mind, sharpening your wits and your pencils for the contest which will begin to-morrow morning in every hall and laboratory of this great University? May I speak for him as I heard him during the winter of 1879-80 from his lecture desk and as he kindly in conversation gave me of his stores of wisdom and experience? May I add from his truly brilliant essays entitled "Science and Education," delivered between 1874 and 1887? May I contribute also from my own thirty-seven years of life as a student and teacher, beginning in 1873 and reaching a turning point in 1910 when Columbia enrolled me among its research professors? It was Huxley's life, his example, the tone of his writings, rather than his actual precepts which most influenced me, for in 1879 he was so intensely absorbed in public work and administration, as well as in research and teaching, that little opportunity remained for laboratory conferences with his students. How I happened to go to him was as follows:

Unlucky—as they appeared to me at the time, but lucky as I look back upon them—were my own early flounderings and blunderings in seeking the true method of education. Huxley has observed of his "Voyage of the Rattlesnake" that it is a good thing to get down to the bare bones of existence. The same is true of self-education. As compared with the hosts of to-day, few men in 1877 knew how to guide the graduate youth; the Johns Hopkins was still nascent; the creative force of Louis Agassiz had spent itself in producing the first school of naturalists, including the genius, William James. One learnt one's errors through falling into pitfalls. With two companions I was guided by a sort of blind instinct to feel that the most important thing in life was to make a discovery of some kind. On consulting one of our most forceful and genial professors his advice was negative and discouraging: "Young men," he said, "go on with your studies for ten or twelve years until you have covered the whole subject; you will then be ready for research of your own." There appeared to be something wrong about this, although we did not know exactly what. We disregarded the advice, left the laboratory of this professor, and at the end of the year did succeed in writing a paper which subsequently attracted the attention of Huxley and was the indirect means of an introduction to Darwin. It was a lame product, but it was ours, and in looking back upon it, one feels with Touchstone in his comment upon Audrey:

> "A poor virgin, Sir,
> An ill favored thing, Sir,
> But mine own."

I shall present in this brief address only one idea, namely, the lesson of Huxley's life and the result of my own experience is that *productive thinking* is the chief *means* as well as the chief *end* of education, and that the natural evolution of education will be to develop this kind of thinking earlier and earlier in the life of the student.

One of the most marvelous of the manifold laws of evolution is what is called '*acceleration.*' By this law the beginning of an important organ like the eye of the chick, for example, is thrust forward into a very early stage of embryonic development. This is, first, because the eye is a very complex organ and needs a long time for development, and second because the fully formed eye of most animals is needed immediately at birth. I predict that the analogy in the evolution of education will be very close. Productive thinking may be compared to the eye; it is needed by the student the moment he graduates, or is hatched, so to speak; it is now developed only in the graduate schools. It is such an integral and essential part of education that the spirit of it is destined to be 'accelerated,' or thrust forward into the opening and preparatory years.

If the lines of one's life were to be cast afresh, if by some metempsychosis one were moulded into what is known as a "great educator," a man of conventions and platforms, and were suddenly to become more or less responsible for 3,000 minds and souls, productive thinking, or the "centrifugal method" of teaching, would not be postponed to graduation or thereafter, but would begin with the Freshman, yes, among these humble men of low estate! It may be *apropos* to recall a story told of President McCosh of Princeton, a man who inspired all his students to production and enlivened them with a constant flow of humor. On one occasion he invited his predecessor, ex-President McLean, to offer prayers in the College Chapel. Dr. McLean's prayer was at once all embracing and reminiscent; it descended from the foreign powers to the heads of the United States government, to the State of New Jersey, through the Trustees, the Faculty, and, in a perfectly logical manner, finally reached the entering class. This naturally raised a great disturbance among the Sophomores, who were evidently jealous of the divine blessing. The disturbance brought the prayer to an abrupt close, and Dr. McCosh was heard to remark: "I should think that Dr. McLean would have more sense than to pray for the Freshmen."

As regards the raw material into which 'productive thinking' is to be instilled, I am an optimist. I do not belong to the 'despair school' of educators, and have no sympathy with the army of editorial writers and prigs who are depreciating the American student. The chief trouble lies not with our youth, nor with our schools, but with our adults. How can springs rise higher than their sources? On the whole, you students are very much above the average American. You are not driven to these doors; certainly in these days of youthful freedom and choice you came of your own free will. The very fact of your coming raises you above the general level, and while you are here you will be living in a world of ideas,—the only kind of a world at all worth living in. You are temporarily cut off more or less from the world of dollars and cents, shillings and pence. Here Huxley helps you in extolling the sheer sense of joy in thinking truer and straighter than others, a kind of superiority which does not mean conceit, the possession of something which is denied the man in the street. You redound with original impulses and creative energy, which must find expression somehow or somewhere; if not under the prevailing incurrent, or 'centripetal system' of academic instruction, it must let itself out in extra-academic activities, in your sports, your societies, your committees, your organizations, your dramatics, all good things and having the highest educational value in so far as they represent your output, your outflow, your centrifugal force.

You are, in fact, in a contest with your intellectual environment outside of these walls. Morally, according to Ferrero, politically, according to Bryce, and economically, according to Carnegie, you are in the midst of a 'triumphant democracy.' But in the world of ideas such as sways Italy, Germany, England, and in the highest degree France, you are in the midst of a 'triumphant mediocrity.' Paris is a city where *ideas* are at a premium and money values count for very little in public estimation. The whole public waits breathlessly upon the production of 'Chanticleer.' That Walhalla of French ambition, 'la Gloire,' may be reached by men of ideas, but not by men of the marts. Is it conceivable that the police of New York should assemble to fight a mob gathered to break up the opera of a certain composer? Is it conceivable that you students should crowd into this theatre to prevent a speaker being heard, as those of the Sorbonne did some years ago in the case of Brunetière? If you should, no one in this city would understand you, and the authorities would be called on promptly to interfere.

A fair measure of the culture of your environment is the depth to which your morning paper prostitutes itself for the dollar, its shades of yellowness, its frivolity or its unscrupulousness, or both. I sometimes think it would be better not to read the newspapers at all, even when they are conscientious, because of their lack of a sense of proportion, in the news columns at least, of the really important things in American life. Our most serious evening mentor of student manners and morals gives six columns to a football game and six lines to a great intercollegiate debate. Such is the difference between precept and practice. American laurels are for the giant captain of industry; when his life is threatened or taken away acres of beautiful forest are cut down to procure the paper pulp necessary to set forth his achievements, while our greatest astronomer and mathematician passes away and perhaps the pulp of a single tree will suffice for the brief, inconspicuous paragraphs which record his illness and death.

Your British cousin is in a far more favorable atmosphere, beginning with his morning paper and ending with the conversation of his seniors over the evening cigar. As a Cambridge man, having spent two years in London and the university, I would not describe the life so much as serious as *worth while*. There are humor and the pleasures of life in abundance, but what is done, is done thoroughly well. Contrast the comments of the British and American press on such a light subject as international polo; the former alone are well worth reading, written by experts and adding something to our knowledge of the game. In the more novel subject of aviation we look in vain in our press for any solid information about construction. Or take the practical subject of politics; the British student finds every great speech delivered in every part of the Empire published in full in his morning paper; as an elector he gets his evidence at first hand instead of through the medium of the editor.

I believe the greatest fault of the American student lies in the over-development of one of his greatest virtues, namely, his collectivism. His strong *esprit de corps* patterns and moulds him too far. The rewards are for the 'lock-step' type of man who conforms to the prevailing ideals of his college. He must parade, he must cheer, to order. Individualism is at a discount; it debars a man from the social rewards of college life. In my last address to Columbia students on the life of Darwin,[1] I asked what would be thought of that peculiar, ungainly, beetle collector if he were to enter one of our colleges to-day? He would be lampooned and laughed out of the exercise of his preferences and predispositions. The mother of a very talented young honor man recently confessed to me that she never spoke of her son's rank because she found it was considered "queer." This is not what young America gen-

[1] Life and Works of Darwin. Pop. Sci. Monthly, Apr., 1909, pp. 315-340. (Address delivered at Columbia University on the one hundredth anniversary of Darwin's birth, as the first of a series of nine lectures on "Charles Darwin and His Influence on Science.")

erates, but what it borrows or reflects from the environment of its elders.

Thus the young American is not lifted up by the example of his seniors, he has to lift it up. If he is a student and has serious ambitions he represents the young salt of his nation, and the college brotherhood in general is a light shining in the darkness. Thus stumbling, groping, often misled by his natural leaders, he does somehow or other, through sheer force, acquire an education, and is just as surely coming to the front in the leadership of the American nation as the Oxford or Cambridge man is leading the British nation.

Our student body is as fine as can be, it represents the best blood and the best impulses of the country; but there may be something wrong, some loss, some delay, some misdirection of educational energy.

Bad as the British university system may be, and it has been vastly improved by the influence of Huxley, it is more effective than ours because more centrifugal. English lads are taught to compose, even to speak in Latin and Greek. The Greek play is an anomaly here, it is an annual affair at Cambridge. There are not one but many active and successful debating clubs in Cambridge.

The faults with our educational design are to be discovered through study of the lives of great men and through one's own hard and stony experience. The best text-books for the nurture of the mind are these very lives, and they are not found in the lists of the pedagogues. Consult your Froebel, if you will, but follow the actual steps to Parnassus of the men whose political, literary, scientific, or professional career you expect to follow. If you would be a missionary, take the lives of Patterson and Livingstone; if an engineer, 'The Lives of Engineers;' if a physician, study that of Pasteur, which I consider by far the noblest scientific life of the nineteenth century; if you would be a man of science, study the recently published lives and letters of Darwin, Spencer, Kelvin, and of our prototype Huxley.

Here you may discover the secret of greatness, which is, first, to be born great, unfortunately a difficult and often impossible task; second, to possess the *instinct of self-education*. You will find that every one of these masters while more or less influenced by their tutors and governors was led far more by a sort of internal, instinctive feeling that they must do certain things and learn certain things. They may fight the battle royal with parents, teachers, and professors, they may be as rebellious as ducklings amidst broods of chickens and give as much concern to the mother fowls, but without exception from a very early age they do their own thinking and revolt against having it done for them, and they seek their own mode of learning. The boy Kelvin is taken to Germany by his father to study the mathematics of Kelland; he slips down into the cellar to the French of Fourier, and at the age of fifteen publishes his first paper to demonstrate that Fourier is right and Kelland is wrong. Pasteur's first research in crystallography is so brilliant that his professor urges him to devote himself to this branch of science, but Pasteur insists upon continuing for five years longer his general studies in chemistry and physics.

This is the true empirical, or laboratory method of getting at the trouble, if trouble there be in the American *modus operandi*; but a generation of our great educators have gone into the question as if no experiments had ever been made. In the last thirty years one has seen rise up a series of 'healers,' trying to locate the supposed weakness in the American student: one finds it in the classic tongues and substitutes the modern; one in the required system and substitutes the elective; one in the lack of contact between teacher and student and brings in preceptors, under whom the patient shows a slight improvement. Now the kind of diagnosis which comes from examining such a life as that of Huxley shows that the real trouble lies in the prolongation to mature years of what may be styled the 'centripetal system,' namely, that afferent, or inflowing mediæval and oriental kind of instruction in which the student is rarely if ever forced to do his own thinking.

You will perceive by this that I am altogether on your side, an insurgent in education, altogether against most of my profession, altogether in sympathy with the over-fed student, and altogether against the prevailing system of overfeeding, which stuffs, crams, pours in, spoon-feeds, and as a sort of deathbed repentance institutes creative work after graduation.

How do you yourself stand on this question? Is your idea of a good student that of a good 'receptacle'? Do you regard your instructors as useful grain hoppers whose duty it is to gather kernels of wisdom from all sources and direct them into your receptive minds? Are you content to be a sort of psychic *Sacculina*, a vegetative animal, your mind a vast sack with two systems, one for the incurrent, the other for the outcurrent of predigested ideas? If so, all your mental organs of combat and locomotion will atrophy. Do you put your faith in reading, or in book knowledge? If so, you should know that not a five foot shelf of books, not even the ardent reading of a fifty foot shelf aided by prodigious memory will give you that enviable thing called culture, because the yardstick of this precious quality is not what you take in but what you give out, and this from the subtle chemistry of your brain must have passed through a mental metabolism of your own so that you have lent something to it. To be a man of culture you need not be a man of creative power, because such men are few, they are born not made; but you must be a man of some degree of centrifugal force, of individuality, of critical opinion, who must make over what is read into conversation and into life. Yes, one little idea of your own well expressed has a greater cultural value than one hundred ideas you absorb; one page that you produce, finely written, new to science or to letters and really worth reading, outweighs for your own purposes the five foot shelf. On graduation, *presto*, all changes, then of necessity must your life be independent and centrifugal; and just in so far as it has these powers will it be successful; just in so far as it is merely imitative will it be a failure.

There is no revolution in the contrary, or outflowing design. Like all else in the world of thought it is, in the germ at least, as old as the Greeks and its illustrious pioneer was Socrates (469-399 B. C.), who led the approach to truth not by laying down the law himself but by means of answers required of his students. The efferent outflowing principle, moreover, is in the program of the British mathematician, Perry and many other reformers to-day.

Against the centripetal theory of acquiring culture Huxley revolted with all his might. His daily training in the centrifugal school was in the genesis of opinion; and he incessantly practiced the precept that forming one's own opinion is infinitely better than borrowing one. Our sophisticated age discourages originality of view because of the plenitude of a ready-made supply of editorials, of reviews, of reviews of reviews, of critiques, comments, translations and cribs. Study political speeches, not editorials about them; read original debates, speeches, and reports. If you purpose to be a naturalist get as soon as you can at the objects themselves; if you would be an artist, go to your models; if a writer, on the same principle take your authors at first hand, and, after you have wrestled with the texts, and reached the full length of your own fathom line, then take the fathom line of the critic and reviewer. Do not trust to mental peptones. Carry the independent, inquisitive, skeptical and even rebellious spirit of the graduate school well down into undergraduate life, and even into school life. If you are a student force yourself to think independently; if a teacher compel your youth to express their own minds. In listening to a lecture weigh the evidence as presented, cultivate a polite skepticism, not affected but genuine, keep a running fire of interrogation marks in your mind, and you will finally develop a mind of your own. Do not climb that mountain of learning in the hope that when you reach the summit you will be able to think for yourself; think for yourself while you are climbing.

In studying the lives of your great men you will find certain of them were veritable storehouses of facts, but Darwin, the greatest of them all in the last century, depended largely upon his inveterate and voluminous powers of note-taking. Thus you may pray for the daily bread of real mental growth, for the future paradise is a state of mind and not a state of memory. The line of thought is the line of greatest resistance; the line of memory is the line of least resistance; in itself it is purely imitative, like the gold or silver electroplating process which lends a superficial coating of brilliancy or polish to what may be a shallow mind.

The case is deliberately overstated to give it emphasis.

True, the accumulated knowledge of what has been thought and said, serves as the gravity law which will keep you from flying off at a tangent. But no warning signals are needed, there is not the least danger that constructive thinking will drive you away from learning; it will much more surely drive you to it, with a deeply intensified reverence for your intellectual forebears; in fact, the eldest offspring of centrifugal education is that keen and fresh appetite for knowledge which springs only from trying to add your own mite to it. How your Maxwell, Herz, Röntgen, Curie, with their world-invigorating discoveries among the laws of radiant matter, begin to soar in your estimation when you yourself wrest one single new fact from the reluctant world of atoms! How your modern poets, Maeterlinck and Rostand, take on the air of inspiration when you would add a line of prose verse to what they are delving for in this mysterious human faculty of ours. Regard Voltaire at the age of ten in 'Louis-le-Grand,' the Eton of France, already producing bad verses, but with a passionate voracity for poetry and the drama. Regard the youthful Huxley returning from his voyage of the 'Rattlesnake' and laying out for himself a ten years' course in search of pure information.

This route of your own to opinions, ideas, and the discovery of new facts or principles brings you back again to Huxley as the man who always had something of his own to say and labored to say it in such a way as to force people to listen to him. His wondrous style did not come easily to him; he himself told me it cost him years of effort, and I consider his advice about style far wiser than that of Herbert Spencer. Why forego pleasures, turn your back on the world, the flesh, and the devil, and devote your life to erudition, observation, and the pen if you remain unimpressive, if you cannot get an audience, if no one cares to read what you write? This moral is one of the first that Huxley has impressed upon you, namely, *write to be read*; if necessary "stoop to conquer," employ all your arts and wiles to get an audience in science, in literature, in the arts, in politics. Get an audience you must, otherwise you will be a cipher and not a force.

Pursuant of the constructive design, the measure of the teacher's success is the degree in which ideas come not from him but from his pupils. A brilliant address may produce a temporary emotion of admiration, a dry lecture may produce a permanent productive impulse in the hearers. One may compare some who are popularly known as gifted teachers to expert swimmers who sit on the bank and talk inspiringly on analyses of strokes; the centrifugal teacher takes the pupils into the water with him, he may even pretend to drown and call for a rescue. In football parlance the coach must get into the scrimmage with the team. This was the lesson taught me by the great embryologist Francis Balfour of Cambridge, who was singularly noted for doing joint papers with his men. An experiment I have tried with marked success in order to cultivate centrifugal power and expression at the same time is to get out of the lecture chair and make my students in turn lecture to me. This is virtually the famous method of teaching law re-discovered by the educational genius of Langdell; the students do all the lecturing and discoursing, the professor lolls quietly in his chair and makes his comments; the stimulus upon ambition and competition is fairly magical; there is in the classroom the real intellectual struggle for existence which one meets in the world of affairs. I would apply this very Socratic principle in every branch of instruction, early and late, and thus obey the 'acceleration' law in education which I have spoken of above as bringing into earlier and earlier stages those powers which are to be actually of service in after life.

There is then no mystery about education if we plan it along the actual lines of self-development followed by these great leaders and shape its deep under-current principles after our own needs and experience. Look early at the desired goal and work toward it from the very beginning. The proof that the secret does not lie in subject, or language, but in preparation for the living productive principle is found in the fact that there have been *relatively* educated men in every stage of history. The wall painters in the Magdalenian caves were the producers and hence the educated men of their day. This goal of production was sought even earlier by the leaders of Eolithic men 200,000 years ago and is equally magnetic for the men of dirigible balloons and aeroplanes of our day. It is, to follow in mind-culture the principle of addition and accretion characteristic of all living things, namely, to develop the highest degree of productive power, centrifugal force, original, creative, individual efficiency. Through this the world advances; the Neolithic man with his invention of polished implements succeeds the Palæolithic, and the man of books and printing replaces the savage.

The standards of a liberal mind are and always have been the same, namely, the sense of Truth and Beauty, both of which are again in conformity with Nature.

> "Beauty is truth, truth beauty, that is all
> Ye know on earth, and all ye need to know."
>
> KEATS' *Ode on a Grecian Urn.*

The sources of our facts are and always have been the same, namely, the learning of what men before you have observed and recorded, and the advance only through the observation of new truth, that is, old to nature but new to man. The handling of this knowledge has always been the same, namely, through human reason. The giving forth of this knowledge and thus the furthering of ideas and customs has and always will be the same, namely, through expression, vocal, written, or manual, that is, in symbols and in design.

It follows that the all round liberally educated man, from Palæolithic times to the time when the earth shall become a cold cinder, will always be the same, namely, *the man who follows his standards of truth and beauty, who employs his learning and observation, his reason, his expression, for purposes of production, that is, to add something of his own to the stock of the world's ideas*. This is the author's conception of a liberal education.

One cannot too often quote the rugged insistence of Carlyle: "Produce! Produce! Were it but the pitifullest infinitesimal fraction of a product, produce it in God's name! 'Tis the utmost thou hast in thee: out with it, then."

Now note that whereas there are the above six powers, namely, truth and beauty, learning and observation, reason, and expression, which subserve the seventh, production or constructive thinking, and whereas the giving out of ideas is the object to be attained, only one power figures prominently in our modern system of college and school education, namely, the learning of facts and the memory thereof. It is no exaggeration to say that this makes up 95% of modern education. Who are the meteors of school and college days? For the most part those with precocious or well trained memories. Why do so many of these meteors flash out of existence at graduation? The answer is simple if you accept my conception of education. Whereas it takes six powers to make a liberally educated man or woman, and seven to make a productive man or woman, only one power has been cultivated assiduously in the 'centripetal' education; whereas there are two great gateways of knowledge, learning and observation, only one has been continuously passed through; whereas there are two universal standards of truth and beauty, only truth has constantly been held up to you, and that in precept rather than in practice. For nothing is surer than this, that the sense of truth must come as a daily personal experience in the life of the student through testing values for himself, as it does in the life of the scientist, the artist, the physician, the engineer, the merchant. Note that whereas you are powerless unless you can by the metabolism of logic make the sum of acquired and observed knowledge your own, that kind of work-a-day efficient logic has never been forced upon you and you are daily, perhaps hourly, guilty of the *non sequitur*, the *post hoc ergo propter hoc*, the 'undistributed middle,' and all those innocent sins against truth which come through the illogical mind.

"That man," says Huxley, "has had a liberal education ... whose intellect is a clear, cold, logic engine, with all its parts of equal strength, and in smooth working order; ready, like a steam-engine, to be turned to any kind of work, and spin the gossamers as well as forge the anchors of the mind."

Note that whereas you are a useless member of society unless you can give forth something of what you know and feel in writing, speaking, or design, your expressive powers may have been atrophied through insufficient use. In brief, you may have shunned individual opinion, observation, logic, expression, because they are each and every one on the lines of greatest resistance. And your teachers not only allowed you but actually encouraged and rewarded you for following the lines of least resistance in the accurate reproduction, in examination papers and marking systems, of their own ideas and those you found in books.

May you, therefore, write down these seven words and read them over every morning: Truth, Beauty, Learning, Observation, Reason, Expression, Production.

In the wondrous old quilt work of inherited, or ancestral predispositions which make your being you may be gifted with all these seven powers in equal and well balanced degree; if you are so blessed you have a great career before you. If, as is more likely, you have in full measure only a part of each, or some in large measure, some in small, keep on the daily examination of your chart as giving you the canons of a liberal education and of a productive mind.

Remember that as regards the somewhat overworked word 'service' every addition in every conceivable department of human activity which is constructive of society is service; that the spirit of science is to transfer something of value from the unknown into the realm of the known, and is, therefore, identical with the spirit of literature; that the moral test of every advance is whether or not it is constructive, for whatever is constructive is moral.

I would not for a moment take advantage of the present opportunity to discourage the study of human nature and of the humanities, but for what is called the best opening for a constructive career let it be Nature.

The ground for my preference is that human nature is an exhaustible fountain of research; Homer understood it well; Solomon fathomed it; Shakespeare divined it, both normal and abnormal; the modernists have been squeezing out the last drops of abnormality.

Nature, studied since Aristotle's time, is still full to the brim; no perceptible falling of its tides is evident from any point at which it is attacked, from nebulæ to protoplasm; it is always wholesome, refreshing, and invigorating. Of the two creative literary artists of our time, Maeterlinck, jaded with human abnormality, comes back to the bee and the flowers and the 'blue bird,' with a delicious renewal of youth, while Rostand turns to the barnyard.

www.ingramcontent.com/pod-product-compliance
Lightning Source LLC
LaVergne TN
LVHW042046070526
838201LV00078B/821